Sunrise and Shorelines: 2001 – 2008

Mark Charlesworth

SUNRISE AND SHORELINES…
2001 – 2008

ISBN 978-1-4092-0029-1

Cover Font designed by Audrius Skersys

Published By
MARK CHARLESWORTH
Preston, Lancashire, United Kingdom

First Edition

Dedicated To:
My mother, Carol Richards; father, Brian Charlesworth; sister, Lauren Charlesworth; and closest friend, Chris Newton

I would also like to thank Denise Hadley for encouraging my interest in English Literature; Martin Griffin for unwavering support when I started out writing; Mike Scott for inspiration; Louise Leddington-Hill for keeping me sane when times were dark; Richie Dawson for web design and technical expertise; my step-dad, Terry Richards, for generously helping to fund the book; and Chris Newton (again) for proof-reading, food, drink, unfaltering friendship and for consistently being here for me in the last 10 years...

IN MEMORY OF MARGARET 'PEGGY' CHARLESWORTH (1927 – 2008): A WONDERFUL MOTHER, GRANDMOTHER AND FRIEND WHO INSPIRED 'A WEARY NIGHT' AND 'THEIR HOME AND THIS HOUSE' http://mark-charlesworth.co.uk

CONTENTS

FOREWORD

I suppose I started writing this book many years ago, even if I didn't know it at the time. I can still picture the scene clearly; the flickering televised footage of aeroplanes crashing into the twin towers, the wreckage blurred in falling dust, the countless unnecessary deaths. September 11th 2001: an event which haunts the world to this day. I was 15, still at high school, and whilst I may have been too young to entirely articulate the general atmosphere of sadness and tragedy in that scarred world, it was an event which inspired me to write nevertheless. The result was a poem named 'America Under Fire', scribbled down whilst still dressed in my school clothes, sat in front of the television watching history change. I guess it was around then that I accidentally started to write this book, now eventually released some 7 years later.

Whilst the earlier works here may not necessarily be sophisticated, this entire collection is written in sincerity. Many of these poems are deeply personal, and this will be the first time some of them have been seen, but part of reason for this book is to exorcise ghosts from the past and move on.

Looking back on this collection (which is printed chronologically) in its entirety, it is noticeable that the mood makes an obvious shift to darker territory. This isn't always fiction. Some works here come from distinctly bleak periods; drinking in the small hours, trying to make sense of everything, and writing in near-darkness to the hauntingly beautiful sounds of Jeff Buckley. There were nights like that when it all felt unreal, unwanted, like watching a shadow of myself on a film-reel. The collection ends, however, with the vaguest hint of hope and optimism.

When spring came, the book was suddenly finished. Having spent months working in front of a computer screen, I decided to head for the river and take advantage of some rare English sunshine. I walked along a tree-lined avenue, past the old Victorian town-houses and down a series of steps until I stumbled upon an amazing panoramic view of the outlands. The whole world seemed to shimmer with a brilliant low-lying mist, the frosty fields glittering under the beautiful sunlight. The river was a million miles below, as though I had arrived at the edge of the world.

Families were walking slowly across the bridge, travellers gazing out as young children paddled in the water. In the distance, birds swooped from the cloudless sky down to the fast-flowing current, and even further a line of hills rose out against the horizon. Above it all, even in the daylight, the moon hung over a line of trees, hovering in the skies like a natural spectre. It seemed inexplicably beautiful that something so heavenly could exist on the edge of an urban hell.

I walked further on to the icy banks, doubling back on myself over the disused railway bridge, to wander along the Victorian promenade. The bare trees formed an arch overhead, their skeletal limbs clawing skywards out of the darkness, but the path was illuminated by lantern-light. To the right was an old statue, and though the path leading towards it appeared to have sunk too far into disrepair, the scene was like stepping back in time.

Further along the banks of the river, clustered houses began to appear, each wonderfully antiquated, old-fashioned and individual. Gradually, it all ebbed back into civilisation. Along the way home, however, the sun hung heavy in the sky, gradually sinking and throwing its beautiful crimson rays upon the industrial wasteland. For a few hours, the world became magnificent once again, despite everything, and I arrived home with a greater sense of hope than I'd ever thought possible over the past year. It was hope for this book, hope for change, and hope for the future…

America Under Fire (September 11th 2001)

The echoing voices feed me the news,
this darkest of days for those who lose
family, friends and lovers dear.
New York's under fire, chaos and tears.

A blackest attack on freedom and liberty,
smoke filled storeys flicker on the TV,
this symbolic corruption of waste and deceit,
the nation sheds a tear through the flames and the heat.

Is the enemy within or on the out?
Political shores watch in sadness and doubt.
Devastation, anarchy, terror and smoke,
Washington under fire, this land desperate and broke.

So how to express this misery of philosophy,
of war, devastation: your false realities.
Living with peace becomes an unreasonable idea,
like abolishing weapons of war and trading this fear.

The Revolt of the Trees (April 2002)

This is the tale of a woodcutter man,
chopped wood in the forest with an axe in his hand,
travelled to market to sell in the town;
the good of the forest hauled by evil hands.

He didn't believe in the power of the land,
no reserves of virtue did he hold in his mind,
chopping trees without mercy to his axe's demand,
to travelling folk he would not be so kind.

And day after day edging through the ground,
the trees looked on to his strong wood house…

Branch by branch they tore it down
to sow the land around with flowers,
and when he got back and saw what they'd done
he reached for his axe, but it was gone.
He gazed in horror to the river where it drowned,
razed to the ground, his home scattered around,
then raised his head towards the sun
and saw what he'd become:
This nightmare, this dream,
Not blood in the stream,
Nor a wave in the sea,
But he stood a tree.

Leaving (September 2003)

A summer dressed in white mist
like no summer before.
And people taken out of time and space
like fate.

The sun shines down
on the green grassy ground,
and the people that sit at the tables.
The music plays on
like a light to your spirit
with a drink, some friends and a song.

The light of the morning
that breaks through the windows
to the ones who're dreaming of the day.
All the world is still,
the houses asleep,
darkness before dawn's shadows creep.

The sound of a fiddle,
a drum and guitar
in a room filled with voices and laughter.
The warm candlelight
reflects in your eyes
to bring people closer together.

But you'll be leaving now,
collecting your life to go.
Home.
It can be easy to forget
when some people move on,
but will there ever be another
summer the same?
Now they're packing their bags one by one.

Now the candle burns thin,
now the people have gone
and will it ever be the same
for the ones who sit and think about
the ones who got away?

Imagination (September 2003)

Ever feel like you can
fall off the edge of the world?
Swim the sands when the tide's
gone out?
Sail in a boat
through the forests below?
Find the space where the grey
of the sea
meets the blue of the sky-
the place that eludes our eye.
Where everything seems to become nothing?
Jump from the highest hill
and fall into the fields below?

Just follow your dream…

Turning to Stone (October 2003)

In search of shelter
you found the place by accident
with a broken down car
and a head that liked to blame the rain.

Tucked away behind a cove of rocks,
and down by stormy shores;
it was quite obvious nobody had been there
for some years before.

The door had to be forced open,
rusted into its hinges from years of decay.
Inside awaited a dark honey-trap, forgotten by time;
old machinery stacked against the wall-sides.
Clockwork probably.
Beyond that, an old light
draped in dust and cobwebs;
useless against the impenetrable shadows of night.
Smashed glass, broken rocks and brickwork
crumbling from the sides of the walls,
now scattered like ashes upon the floor.

Then it loomed from the gloom up ahead,
a creaking spiral staircase,
the promise of an old mattress or bed.

Well, it's just that same old story-
the one that everyone knows.
The one about the lighthouse keeper
who fell asleep
and turned to stone.

Buried Things (November 2003)

One by one;
forgotten, scattered, abandoned without a sound,
mismatched, worthless items that fell to the ground.

An old lady's bejewelled brooch,
once treasured, passed down as a family heirloom,
now passed away in the cold, misty gloom.
A bag of coins – old currency –
worthless now, stripped of sentimentality.
The ruby red stone of a wedding ring,
one of three, *not worth a bloody thing*.
A stone with a carving,
the fruit of forgotten toil,
misplaced, dead, trampled in the soil.

And in the course of passing seasons,
lying lost, devoid of reason,
these treasures no longer of human worth
began to grow shoots deep into the earth,
branches and roots accidentally sown.
When springtime came, there flowers did grow.

That humans will squander, whittle and waste
means little against the blood of the age.
These are items immortal within progress' line
yet we are merely ghosts drifting through time.

Six Months Later (February 2004)

The hazy mist that turns to dust
and falls to the ground,
carpeting the lawns in cold grey
like a frost.

These winter streets seem lonely now
feeling this melancholy sorrow
as I pass time with the one companion
who won't leave.

Even walking up the hill
to see the sun,
the world looks dull,
the clouds a cotton white,
the streets below a distant place.

Somehow, it feels as though the heart
has been ripped away from here
and there's nobody around to talk to,
so it seems right to put it to the back of my mind-
make the best of it.
Washed away by beer, wine, rum and the company of a close friend
who probably understood better than anybody else,
prepared to listen and see it through to the end.

It should have ended right back then.
I should have left, never to revisit that place again
until my heart saw fit to bring me back,
because right now the silence echoes painfully
and all I can think is
'it's funny how things change in such a short time,
and just how inadequate is the beer, rum and wine!'

Home by the Sky (March 2004)

It seemed strangely vivid,
that hazy crimson light,
through the new spring leaves,
where evening sleepwalks into night.

In the distance things are growing dark
as a million heads hit pillows
and dream of travellers in places far,
but right here the wood-smoke billows.

I whispered to myself:
I'll be happy with the deep blue
that fills a space on the horizon.
…and I meant it too.

Cause there's a place in between
here and there
where the crimson meets the ocean
tipped by shades of black.

In the distance
some far away suburban lights
cast electric shadows
onto those who managed to get away

…only to come back…

On the horizon
the white crescent
rises majestically above a hill
capped by snow, or leaves, or stones-
shrouded figures in dark celebration.

Far away
waves crash gently across a rocky shore
where shadows stroll in the dark
looking for the distant lights of home
surrounded by trees,
at the foot of a hill
or maybe by ruined towers in the woods.

But for these peaceful moments
I lie in waiting for what comes next
as the sky deepens its melancholy shade.

Alcoholic's Corner (April 2004)

Gypsies, poets, vagabonds,
the songs they sung,
the smoky lungs.
Beneath the bleary eyes
in a world
a world apart
that's now so gone.

The ghosts are lingering by the bar
as a thousand voices
fade into one.
The ever imposing silence,
the rust
and the rot.
Spare a penny for the drinkers that time forgot.

'This is a god-awful place;
we cling on, we survive.
The drink robs our dignity'
and then we die…

Every day
and all the while,
when we're too tired to force a smile,
we call a round again,
last stop before the grave,
and try to forget all we could've done with our lives.

Tall Tales (April 2004)

I saw a cat's tail
curl round the moon.
I saw hell's flames
in a sleepy lake.
I saw a tall tree
telling a tale
to a broken old man
at his own wake.

I saw a shadow
that danced in my eyes
like a trick of the light.
I saw an owl
that was smoking a pipe
and speaking words to the wise.

I saw a creature that lived in the rocks,
I saw a god in human form,
I saw the moon had the face of a clock,
I saw the devil, his gaze forlorn.

I saw an idol made from twigs,
I saw a horseman dressed in black.
The tale's told he's in dark service
and has been to hell and back.

I saw a girl dressed in pyjamas
climbing a ladder to the stars.
I saw, clearly, every age
That befell this earth before.

I saw what hides.
On that night
I saw the other side.

Fairy Tales (May 2004)

Once upon a time
I tripped over a root
and found myself face down
in a glassy puddle
where I saw a thousand faces
reaching out,
dragging me down to another age.

It would seem as though
I was a different person then-
so much the same
and still so much changed,
but I found myself in a place
where I walked
hand in hand with my own past.

And just what was it
these visions of time,
lain side by side,
sought to show me?

This fairy tale,
this place
where a mirror no longer reveals a reflection
but a series of disjointed images,
fading in an out like memories,
descending into ripples
where they wither and die.

Once upon a time I chose the past,
for the memories that it holds,
but the curtain lows, the darkness grows
and the future seems so cold.

Silent Prayer (June 2004)

What the fuck do we do now?
Torn between truth and lies,
does anyone know,
who tells the most convincing tale
and who's wearing the honest disguise?

I write this
caught between the one who'll console me
and the one who'll insult me.
Misjudged apologies, implicitly fake
and far too late.

And what of the fucking
Cheshire cat grin,
knife sticking in, bastard
on the other side?
Relish their misery before it dies.

'Of course, we're bound to be paranoid.
It's symptomatic of the twenty-first century.'
I write this in blood,
the colour of wine.
These tears pour out in darkest night.

So, when you next drain the bottle,
which turns every man into all they really are,
don't dare fuck up my family
and leave a bloody scar!

The Forest Awakened (May 2005)

I took shelter in the forest
when the rainstorm began,
travelling in a lonely place,
devoid of human hand.

The hills in the distance
ran with rivers of ice
slowly cascading
into the heart of the night.

The first part of the journey
had been hindered by sun.
Now I took my comfort
when the rain had begun

so I rode to the place
where time seemed to fade
and the leaves of the trees
grew in all different shades.

Some planes grew red,
and some planes grew gold.
Some leaves had turned brown,
others withered and old.

The forest dressed in splendour
and laced in the sun,
the elegant blossoms
speak of spring-times gone.

And amidst all this life, the place seemed still,
silent and elegant, the sensuous thrill.

I encountered a clearing where the blossoms grew thick
and soon the rain was just a distant memory,
where now, small crystalline droplets
fell through the leaves
that gave me a shelter,
so away I could steal.

I had crouched on a rock
in the circle of trees,
which surrounded the place,
as though watching in wait.

Somewhere, here and there,
blackness crept in,
mere shards of light,
as though the darkness could sing.
I felt as though lost under moonlit sky,
no longer aware of the passing of time.

I reached in my pocket
for a match and a light.
Illumination flooded
and it was then I realised,
a cryptic message before my eyes:
'talk not of reality,
and a distance of truth,
of things you can touch
and things you can prove.
Consider imagination,
consider the land,
envisage the sea
and call to the trees.
For though you've walked on burning stones,
through times torturous and dark,
you are not alone, your closest desire never too far'.

So I held up a light
to the trees ahead,
where the path journeyed on.
I saw not a bark,
but a woman's head,
branches that gave way to arms.

Her fingers like spider-webs,
hair glowing starlight,
a sparkling wisdom within her dark eyes.

This lady approached,
all dressed in white,
and silk which reflected
the cold night sky.

Where the leaves had been
of the old oak tree,
now grew her long, fair hair.

She raised her head
and called to me
in a wordless whisper,
her voice like running water, soft and clear.

And then she began to turn her back,
walking slowly into the black,
star lit, scarlet darkness up ahead.

I cannot say why, as I now tell my tail,
but I found myself chasing her snowy white trail.
Her silken robes glittered in the dark,
to beckon me on when I strayed too far.

Her forest seemed to breathe with life,
the goddess radiating the place with light;
rushing water in the distant streams,
a gentle breeze caressing the trees,
the sorrowful creaking of branches and roots,
reinvigorating the rotting fruit.

It was then that the darkness ended,
and she stopped still
in a place of great height,
trees clawing for light.
They savoured such heavenly salvation,
devouring the moonlight which poured,
hot nectar into their very hearts.

The girl opened her mouth as though to speak,
the woodlands breathing her every breath,
the water, leaves, trees and breeze,
and I alone understood her.

As she threw her arms around me,
I felt my roots stretching deeper than ever I thought they could,
reaching into the river, I was at last alive.
I was in love.

She left me there,
literally rooted to the spot.
She was gone to a distant place
but her tale I never forgot.

I smiled, though in regret,
and realised I had returned
to where my journey had begun.
Now how the world was alive!
The darkness overcome.

Left astray on the rocks,
I reached for the map,
but I'd found that home,
found that soul,
so away it was cast.

I looked to the place
where the girl had first been,
and beheld the most beautiful tree I ever had seen.

I waited there forever after,
such was I transfixed by the beauty of the enchanted oak,
no fear for the world I'd forsaken.
I was the forest
and she was awakened.

To Watch the Storms (July 2005)

To watch the storms
across the hillsides,
to see the place
where time collides.

To rejoice
at the point of mid-summer,
in the warm black night
and the dark red wine.

Scattered people
stare down
from summer gardens
across the violent sea,
repeating the dance
of the skies above,
throwing torment
to the shores.

Across the far banks
where a train makes its way
across the land,
a mere fleeting shadow
against the endless
stretch of hills.

Across from distant motorways
where cars drive at speed
through lake-side
quarries and landfills.

All taking part
in the vivid dance
across the sky,
like watching the storms
in green hill-sides.

The Final Days of Summer (September 2005)

The flies feed
on the fallen autumn fruit,
sweet nectar
bursts from cracked brown skin.

The flowers fall,
the petals wilt,
the ripened seed
breaks free within.

The hallows harvest,
the fields are still,
the black crows circle
the silent hill,

so, turn on the lights
in this darkest sky,
burn the candle-wick
and stoke up the fire.

Diminished by time,
trees fall to sleep,
the summer nights
must come to cease

until such time
as light prevails,
and the earth awakes
from a winter's tale.

Come the Floods (October 2005)

Come the floods of the sixteenth year,
come the swirling mists of morn,
alive with hope, aghast in fear
comes the traveller in the storm.

Echoing throughout the valley,
came the rumour of distant war.
The clattering steel of swords and armour
crafted in the blacksmith's forge.

Come with me on the great journey
through history, myth and mystery,
to a land most mystical
but troubled by mankind.

Come with me to lands of autumn,
and the answers we shall find,
come the floods of buried pasts,
echoes of a distant time.

Strange City (October 2005)

They held you in shackles on the night that you died,
your screams ran through streets of the city.
They swore that you cried tears of blood from your eyes,
while old men spat anger or pity.

So how does it feel to be falsely accused
of a murder you did not commit?
And how does it feel to be beaten and bruised
while your life slips away as you see it?

And when you awoke, how you wept for their lies,
to pay someone else's penance.
Left all alone in a cellar to die,
but you swore that you'd have your vengeance…

So how does it feel when you suffer for them,
victim to the noose where you fell?
Ghosts to the conscience of the bloodthirsty men,
you'll see that they're rotting in hell.

You chased over cobbles, and whispered in their ears,
drove them to guilt and played on their fears,
till the last took a knife lest his soul should be saved,
but he lies with the devil, not rests in the grave.

Alone (November 2005)

An almost empty glass,
a faded, withered rose.
I found the candle wick burnt down,
I find myself sat here alone.

I stand silent in autumn stillness,
and strum a sombre tone,
I watch the stars, take in their beauty,
inertia creeps, division grows.

At the waters edge in darkest night,
waiting to go home,
I watch the light throw silent shadows
and cast a sorry stone.

So, in the warm and dusky inns
the day draws to a close
I dream of love I may never find,
And turn to leave alone…

End of the Earth (January 2006)

Sirens scream down silent streets
and tear the night apart,
broken earth beneath your feet
and a dagger through your heart.

Swaying branches call their song
for the lonely and the lost,
the blackest souls seek retribution
to face the penance and the cost.

The lovers share their final breath
alone in one another's arms,
a weeping mother rocks a child,
in shelter from the violent storm.

Figures rise, entombed from the past,
the devil's dance, a raucous laugh,
to chink their goblets and raise the glass,
and toast the shadows mankind has cast.

And when it comes unto the last,
a wise old man with felt brimmed hat,
he drains the barrel and slams the door,
'to the ends of this earth, my dear, and many more!'

The Wanderer (February 2006)

A serpent in a stained glass window,
a name upon a weathered grave.
Scribbled in a black book in my pocket
is a risk I didn't take
and a game I didn't play.

A child rocking slowly in a cradle,
a cloaked figure lurking at the gate.
A ghost sits waiting as the past catches up
from a hand dealt by fate,
choices taken in haste.

The cellar door stands open,
a hand beckons down from below,
to wander blind into the darkness,
and risk to choke,
the traveller must go.

A future facing indecision,
or a blind man's paradise.
The wanderer seeks a promise to keep,
or else be withered by time
at the turning of the tide.

Possessed (April 2006)

You were cold as death
when they found you,
you were rocking in your bed
so they bound you.

They set a watch inside your room,
hung a cross where flowers bloomed
locked you in your sorry tomb,
for this child is possessed.

You screamed aloud a cursed name,
forbade you speaking of the pain,
your dress that is with blood stained,
for 'this is what is best'.

To cut away the darkest spirits,
that scream inside your head,
and wash away the creaking boards
where you slowly bled.

They set you loose one autumn day,
the breeze that blows your matted hair,
they found her body in the water
and cried out loud it wasn't fair

for she was taken in your name
you dreamt in darkest night,
sat alone in mortal shame
unable to face the daylight…

And you were cold as death
when she found you,
you were screaming your regret
when she drowned you.

Cast a shadow on a family of lies,
the fallen cross where the flowers died,
and not a single tear was cried
for the man they called possessed.

Dead Leaves (November 2006)

Dead leaves drift in mid-summer,
the seasons turned too soon,
the wrath of cold November,
the chilling winter moon.

The solemn tide of black-water,
under starry skies,
lone ship on the bleak horizon,
seeking distant fires.

They came, they saw,
they left their names,
and took this land for granted,
to play their sorry games.
The trees they tore
from a land in pain,
but this night they won't sleep easy,
to pay for the earth's bane.

Hand in hand on polluted sands,
the weeds struggled to life,
dragged their roots to crawl ashore,
seek the slayer and his knife.

Run to distant churchyards,
but absolution won't save,
when every victim of human hands
will rise from 'neath their grave

to slay the darkest sinners,
the righteous ones they crave,
these ghosts from the past, their shadows cast,
to pillage and purge this age.

From the Heart (February 2007)

I'd love to leave and let you be
but in your arms you hold my heart
to open with a rusty key,
the swaying cradle in the dark.

The candle that will always burn,
the moths that dance for flickering flames,
and as the lock so slowly turns
temptation conceals a world of pain.

I'd love to show you how I feel,
to tear away this heart that bleeds,
beating in the black of night,
dark angel wings to soft moonlight.

But in the end, we wrapped in cloth,
the bloody organ, the wooden box,
draped in silk, veiled in pain
until you break my heart again…

Kendal Castle (June 2007)

The blood of ages lay heavy in the sky,
a beautiful witch in a whore's disguise,
a tale of sorcery, deception and lust,
now the armour and sword has gone to rust.

Dusk is falling on the town at night,
industrial decadence for a madman's plight,
walls of stone swept away in a flood,
grandeur to ashes and splendour to dust.

A moonlit glint, lone star shines bright,
the world was rebuilt in the blink of an eye.
A new beauty shines in another great age
to stand time's test 'gainst the wars we wage.

Now shadows fall in Kendal town,
a world weary folk-tale as the castle looks down,
where red wine's spilt instead of blood long ago,
the bustling streets and the cigarette smoke…

The Last Temptation of Leonard Black (July 2007)

The rain-drenched fool stepped out from the dark,
where the fiddlers and devil's folk drank together in bars.
A holy man he, preached damnation and hell
'till he descended the steps of the gypsy hotel.

With walls stained in blood, no stranger should pass,
there a dark woman sat, draining her red wine glass.
He succumbed to her temptation, debauchery so low
for that was the night Leonard Black sold his soul.

He tore up the scriptures, the paintings and pictures,
from hell no way back, dearly damned Leonard Black.

He went to see a priest, but the blind fool cried
that alcohol and devilry had surely warped his mind,
so he turned on his heel, no confession of sin,
he had to take a leap of faith for the trouble he was in.

He tore through the land with a knife in his hand,
from hell no way back, dearly damned Leonard Black,
he ran through the streets, the rain covered his tracks,
his cries rang through the land, but nobody called back:

Hallowed demons beseech my soul tonight!
Hallowed demons beseech my soul tonight!
I hope that you'll forgive me my dark plight,
I shall absolve my shadowy sins come midnight

The temptress she lay, sprawled on her back,
Naked and bloody from Black's vengeful wrath.
The knife he cast by the old river banks
"I carry out the work of Christ!" cried the holy man.

The body they found, covered in dirt,
sign of the cross etched into her flesh.
A man dressed in priest's robes, or so they heard,
spoke "here lies a sinner and we are blessed by her death".

Broken Man (December 2007)

A plate of crumbs, a dim-lit tree,
an unmade bed, cold cup of tea.
By the flickering television screen
the broken man sits and screams.

No-one knew him, they couldn't see,
cursèd invisibility,
when he cried out they couldn't hear,
trapped in four walls, cold whispers near.

Can anyone hold me, love me, hear me, feel me,
if you fear me, heal me, be near me, help me
for I am forever lost.

This room so cold, the blood I drew,
one way window where eyes peer through.
By the flickering computer screen
a broken man, and a wasted year.

(…and the note read…)

No-one held me, loved me, heard me, felt me,
healed me, neared me, saw me, helped me.
Now I am forever lost.

The body found, the men recoiled,
he was left to rot in the sullied soil,
disfigured appearance, a missing hand,
butterfly collector or broken man?

They broke him, choked him, stalk him, taunt him,
he was not a man like any other,
and now he is forever gone.

Evensong (December 2007)

Two-zero-zero-seven: that terrible year,
4am: unable to sleep, the shadows creep,
whiskey, wine, a state of perpetual fear,
alcohol to pacify, conceal the hidden deep.

Everything uprooted, an axe crashes down:
it felt like burying the hatchet in this sleepy town,
so with everything gone, nothing to do but run,
to fix the smile with thumb-screws and turn from the sun.

We left it all behind, but there was nowhere to hide,
before we knew it, we were as shadows in the night.
Break down, new town; no job, no love, no home,
security gave way to surveillance, horror from hope.

Time to start again, break free from these chains,
crawl from this hole and run through the rain,
give me a chance, two-zero-zero-eight,
from these bleeding wounds I'll be born again.

This is the evensong,
a world that I don't belong,
a song that I shouldn't have wrote,
a premature suicide note.
She drove me away,
but I'll return to this stage,
momentarily lost
so we all pay the cost.
To flee from the fire, and relinquish that fear
of two-zero-zero-seven: that terrible year.

The Magnolia Room (December 2007)

The first thing they noticed in the sleeping tomb
was a fragrant scent and a rose in bloom.
They studied by candle light and felt for a lamp,
then on closer inspection the petals were black.
This place told of riches, for which a jealous fool would kill;
artefacts, treasures, antiques draped in silk.
The clock and the pendulum lurked in the gloom,
both stopped in respect like the stone dead full moon.
It peered through the window and threw an eerie light,
upon the magnolia room keeper's demise.
A figure, ambiguous by its androgyny, sat perfectly still,
no breath and no heartbeat, somehow exquisitely thrilled.
Surely not by the noose that hung round its neck?
A nightmare illuminated by this strangest of deaths.
The clothes given life by magnolia spice,
and a tear of blood running down from one eye.

Sail Away (January 2008)

When Christmas came
a man walked through the rain
in a town that he hardly knew.
Fairy lights twinkled
in old shop windows
like the glint of that beautiful moon.

Up the creaking steps
with the dispossessed,
his wishes he expressed,
and though they shook their heads,
he swore he caught a smile
for the romance he'd confessed.

The strange old man travelled
from town to town,
dressed in his black suit,
and through the streets he ran,
dreamed of his retirement plan,
and thc glint of that bcautiful moon.

That Christmas long ago
he returned from the snow
to his sleepy suburban home.
There waited his wife
dressed for a flight,
their bags packed in her weeks alone.

They collected the cat,
scribbled a note,
and blew out the candle in their room,
locked up the door
and left for the shore
for the glint of that beautiful moon.

The boat was tethered,
on the old pebble beach,
waiting for three shadows of night.
They boarded in silence,
a smile on their face,
drank wine by the pale lunar light.

As they left for the stars
he whispered in her ear
'I bought you the moon, and I love you'.
It was 1938
when they sailed away,
on course for the magnificent moon.

Now people still stare
for that elderly pair,
in search of the boat in the sky.
It was the strangest folk-tale
I ever did hear,
in *The Sail Away Inn* late one night.

Captured (January 2008)

We put it back, that photograph,
instamatic holiday snap,
your make-up cracked,
stray cigarette ash.
Crimson lips, this divine whore,
swore she always wanted more
than smoky halls
and yellow walls. 'Is that all?'

It seemed like heaven, that moment of hell,
now the photograph itself is unwell.
The gloss it peels, the smoke grows thick,
the cancerous lung, the heart so sick.

This picture was taken one year ago,
captured, seized, knifed in the throat.
I cannot take the past away,
the image lives to fight the day.
I can smell the perfume you used to keep,
now sickeningly ill and cheap.
Goodnight whore, these words are dead,
though I hope you sleep sound in your bed.

A Weary Night (January 2008)

Forget who you were.
Forget who you are.
For one night the world is a magical place
where every name and every face,
shadows you once knew,
shall meet by the light of the full moon.

Every friend and every lover,
ghosts, lost family, those undiscovered
will find their way to the same old shore,
perhaps by chance or something more,
a meeting devised by fortuitous fate
when the hour is growing late.

The figures of many a distant memory
you thought you'd dwelled upon too much,
those spectral spirits of the past
once again gathered together
…at last.

Come now everyone,
walk to the shore, we have begun.
A boatman waits,
through the water to wade
to a house lit by candles.
For tonight we shall stay.

And when the morning comes to steal you away,
and we pass in sorrow this weariest of days,
time will not rob us that memory
of that beautiful night when you were still here.

You left your mark in our minds and hearts,
but in tearful sorrow we must now come to part.

Their Home and This House (January 2008)

Silent and empty, this sorrowful house,
melancholy as autumn and absent of sound,
sombre and sober, a man sits alone
picking through the memories of his old home:
the magazine stack, a box of old photographs,
the disconnected line of an antiquated telephone;
cabinets of glass, assorted old bric-a-brac,
a pile of Sunday papers stacked neatly in the rack.

Then in December the dates all but stopped,
the mail collected inside the letterbox,
stained dishes sat, the washing untouched,
the shimmering ornaments now covered in dust.
The music is over, but the vinyl still cracks,
you slipped away when we turned our backs.
The nineteen-forties record player ceased its song
as if in respect, now that you're gone.

Theirs was home to a family, but the clocks have all stopped,
this house a museum, now that her heart is lost.

Coming Back to Life (February 2008)

It was the rain that woke him from eternal sleep,
the comatose, nocturnal deep,
found in an empty hospital ward
littered with newspapers, tattered and torn.

The edge of the walls felt like the end of the world,
there corridors whispered stories of old;
the window-ledge undusted, the iron bedstead rusted.
He strayed to the shadows that seemed to sorrowfully call.

Wandering alone up the Victorian steps,
intense humming silence, a claustrophobic effect:
more chilling by far than the presence of death,
no drips, no bleeps nor cries in this wreck,

but an eerie sense pervaded nevertheless,
icy fingers that ran down his neck;
all sweetness and sincerity drained
like petals crushed in the winter rain.

Shadows and spectres where he couldn't flee them;
a solitary prisoner in a glass mausoleum,
a thousand reflections to drive a knife in his back
till under force of his weight the mirror did crack.

Fleeing from the shadow of that ruinous wreck,
the concrete turned to earth with each hurried step,
'till worn and torn he gave in and slept
and woke where the air wasn't stale, but fresh.

He was struck by the sensuous perfume-like scent,
the blood dripped flowers of scarlet and red,
he was lost in the space of the misty green haze,
the allure of the forest like forbidden love's gaze.

Travelling revealed beauty in this place he'd arrived;
mountainous cliffs, both terrible and sublime,
storms that were fearsome but a gift to the eyes,
expansive orchards yielding bittersweet wine,

a field of orchids turned poisonous and wild,
the sweet rain falling like the tears he cried,
for when things grew lonely in the forest he'd hide,
but the forest grew darker with each passing night.

No stars in the sky, no light from the moon;
this could be heaven or hell in perpetual gloom,
so was this his rebirth or was this his tomb?
Had he cheated death or escaped far too soon?

When he came to the sea that was basked in dawn's light,
the veil was lifted and he realised:
this world was created entirely for him, no other survivor,
no more human beings.

No birds, insects, bees, no shadows that stalked,
a murmuring breeze but no voices to talk.
So what good is heaven, if heaven's being alone?
To possess an empty kingdom as a king without a throne?

There beauty meant nothing against the calling of home,
and a fairy-tale forest is but a nightmare unknown.
This world seemed so cold when nobody spoke,
of the sunrise, shorelines and suicide notes.

So here I am, trapped inside a perfect world,
miraculously alive on the day that I died,
my snow-globe, my Eden, this lonely paradise.
I cling onto the vaguest hope that I'm coming back to life…

www.ingramcontent.com/pod-product-compliance
Ingram Content Group UK Ltd.
Pitfield, Milton Keynes, MK11 3LW, UK
UKHW041835200726
13854UKWH00003BA/1156